THE ROSAR

A VISUAL AID FOR PRAYING THE ROSARY

"Abundant Divine Blessings upon all associated"
Pope John Paul II

THE ROSARY

What is the Rosary? Originally it was simply a counting device made up of knots or beads on a piece of string. Over the centuries, the Rosary has evolved to become the most universal form of Mary prayer, involving touch, sight and sound. It was once a prayer necklace of 15 sets of beads arranged in groups of 10 – a decade – corresponding to fifteen episodes in and about Christ's life. Five for joy, five for sorrow, and five for glory. (Today five decades is considered as a Rosary.) Mary said "Your will be done" and in the Rosary God's will is done beautifully. *So as we pray the Rosary we walk through Christ's life with Mary,* for it contains Mary as mother, sister, friend and guide in, with and through Christ.

Mary herself recommended this prayer at Lourdes (1858), Fatima (1917), and now at Medjugorge where, since 1981, she has appeared carrying a Rosary. Time honoured, familiar and warm, it is a marvellous antidote to the darkness and desperation of our world.

THE ROSARY FOR TODAY

Can we overdo this Mary business? Yes. But the real danger is underdoing it. The reformation rejected Mary. But she has returned to be loved and honoured by many Christians along with the Muslims, who have always revered her.

Mary is, after all God's choice of mother for Christ and one of God's greatest gifts. In turn, the Rosary is, under God, one of Mary's most precious gifts to us. Mary for so long a symbol of division among Christians has become for many a sign of our unity.

Get hold of the Rosary and it will get hold of you. First we get used to the feel of the beads, the Rosary then begins to release us into prayer in the heart as well as in the head, it only 'comes alive' by actually praying it. It helps us on the way in every facet of life.

A ROSARY WAY

A Rosary Way is but a new and exciting dimension to an already ageless form of prayer; by means of sculptures, erected on a walk way, or in a garden, the 15 episodes of the Rosary are made visible and presented to our senses and hearts.

A LIVING ROSARY

Early in the nineteenth century Pauline Jaricot – the founder of the A.P.F. – The Association of the Propagation of the Faith – saw the revival of the Rosary as a tool in the winning back of France to God, "I was convinced that the mere distribution of alms, and pious books would produce no good fruit unless accompanied by prayer, and it seemed to me that it would please God if we could have recourse to this ancient practice." Her method was to divide the Rosary between groups of 15 persons. Each member would say one decade every day taking the various mysteries in turn to form a Living Rosary. By using this little book and saying a decade of the Rosary each one of us can become part of a Living Rosary in the world praying for the world.

THE ANNUNCIATION

THE JOYFUL MYSTERIES

THE ANNUNCIATION (Luke 1: 26–38)

In the sixth month the angel Gabriel was sent by God to a town in Galilee called Nazareth, to a virgin betrothed to a man named Joseph, of the House of David; and the virgin's name was Mary. He went in and said to her, 'Rejoice, so highly favoured! The Lord is with you.' She was deeply disturbed by these words and asked herself what this greeting could mean, but the angel said to her, 'Mary, do not be afraid; you have won God's favour. Listen! You are to conceive and bear a son, and you must name him Jesus. He will be great and will be called Son of the Most High. The Lord God will give him the throne of his ancestor David; he will rule over the House of Jacob for ever and his reign will have no end.' Mary said to the angel, 'But how can this come about, since I am a virgin?' 'The Holy Spirit will come upon you' the angel answered 'and the power of the Most High will cover you with its shadow. And so the child will be holy and will be called Son of God. Know this too: your kinswoman Elizabeth has, in her old age, herself conceived a son, and she whom people called barren is now in her sixth month, for nothing is impossible to God.' 'I am the handmaid of the Lord,' said Mary 'let what you have said be done to me.' And the angel left her.

THE VISITATION

THE VISITATION (Luke 1: 39–56)

Mary set out at that time and went as quickly as she could to a town in the hill country of Judah. She went into Zechariah's house and greeted Elizabeth. Now as soon as Elizabeth heard Mary's greeting, the child leapt in her womb and Elizabeth was filled with the Holy Spirit. She gave a loud cry and said, 'Of all women you are the most blessed, and blessed is the fruit of your womb. Why should I be honoured with a visit from the mother of my Lord? For the moment your greeting reached my ears, the child in my womb leapt for joy. Yes, blessed is she who believed that the promise made her by the Lord would be fulfilled.'

THE MAGNIFICAT

And Mary said:
'My soul proclaims the greatness of the Lord
and my spirit exults in God my saviour;
because he has looked upon his lowly handmaid.
Yes, from this day forward all generations will call me blessed,
for the Almighty has done great things for me.
Holy is his name,
and his mercy reaches from age to age for those who fear him.
He has shown the power of his arm,
he has routed the proud of heart.
He has pulled down princes from their thrones and exalted the lowly.
The hungry he has filled with good things, the rich sent empty away.
He has come to the help of Israel his servant, mindful of his mercy
– according to the promise he made to our ancestors –
of his mercy to Abraham and to his descendants for ever.'
Mary stayed with Elizabeth about three months and then went back home.

THE NATIVITY

THE NATIVITY (Luke 2: 1–20)

Now at this time Caesar Augustus issued a decree for a census of the whole world to be taken. This census – the first – took place while Quirinius was governor of Syria, and everyone went to his own town to be registered. So Joseph set out from the town of Nazareth in Galilee and travelled up to Judaea, to the town of David called Bethlehem, since he was of David's House and line, in order to be registered together with Mary, his betrothed, who was with child. While they were there the time came for her to have her child, and she gave birth to a son, her first-born. She wrapped him in swaddling clothes, and laid him in a manger because there was no room for them at the inn. In the countryside close by there were shepherds who lived in the fields and took it in turns to watch their flocks during the night. The angel of the Lord appeared to them and the glory of the Lord shone round them. They were terrified, but the angel said, 'Do not be afraid. Listen, I bring you news of great joy, a joy to be shared by the whole people. Today in the town of David a saviour has been born to you; he is Christ the Lord. And here is a sign for you: you will find a baby wrapped in swaddling clothes and lying in a manger.' And suddenly with the angel there was a great throng of the heavenly host, praising God and singing:

'Glory to God in the highest heaven,
and peace to men who enjoy his favour'.

Now when the angels had gone from them into heaven, the shepherds said to one another, 'Let us go to Bethlehem and see this thing that has happened which the Lord has made known to us'. So they hurried away and found Mary and Joseph, and the baby lying in the manger. When they saw the child they repeated what they had been told about him, and everyone who heard it was astonished at what the shepherds had to say. As for Mary, she treasured all these things and pondered them in her heart. And the shepherds went back glorifying and praising God for all they had heard and seen; it was exactly as they had been told.

THE PRESENTATION

THE PRESENTATION (Luke 2: 22–39)

And when the day came for them to be purified as laid down by the Law of Moses, they took him up to Jerusalem to present him to the Lord – observing what stands written in the Law of the Lord: Every first-born male must be consecrated to the Lord – and also to offer in sacrifice, in accordance with what is said in the Law of the Lord, a pair of turtle doves or two young pigeons. Now in Jerusalem there was a man named Simeon. He was an upright and devout man; he looked forward to Israel's comforting and the Holy Spirit rested on him. It had been revealed to him by the Holy Spirit that he would not see death until he had set eyes on the Christ of the Lord. Prompted by the Spirit he came to the Temple; and when the parents brought in the child Jesus to do for him what the Law required, he took him into his arms and blessed God; and he said:

THE NUNC DIMITTIS

'Now, Master, you can let your servant go in peace, just as you promised; because my eyes have seen the salvation which you have prepared for all the nations to see, a light to enlighten the pagans and the glory of your people Israel'.

THE PROPHECY OF SIMEON

As the child's father and mother stood there wondering at the things that were being said about him, Simeon blessed them and said to Mary his mother, 'You see this child: he is destined for the fall and for the rising of many is Israel, destined to be a sign that is rejected – a sword will pierce your own soul too – so that the secret thoughts of many may be laid bare'.

THE PROPHECY OF ANNA

There was a prophetess also, Anna the daughter of Phanuel, of the tribe of Asher. She was well on in years. Her days of girlhood over, she had been married for seven years before becoming a widow. She was now eighty-four years old and never left the Temple, serving God night and day with fasting and prayer. She came by just at that moment and began to praise God; and she spoke of the child to all who looked forward to the deliverance of Jerusalem.

THE HIDDEN LIFE OF JESUS AT NAZARETH

When they had done everything the Law of the Lord required, they went back to Galilee, to their own town of Nazareth. Meanwhile the child grew to maturity, and he was filled with wisdom; and God's favour was with him.

FINDING THE CHILD JESUS IN THE TEMPLE

FINDING THE CHILD JESUS IN THE TEMPLE (Luke 2: 41–52)

Every year his parents used to go to Jerusalem for the feast of the Passover. When he was twelve years old, they went up for the feast as usual. When they were on their way home after the feast, the boy Jesus stayed behind in Jerusalem without his parents knowing it. They assumed he was with the caravan, and it was only after a day's journey that they went to look for him among their relations and acquaintances. When they failed to find him they went back to Jerusalem looking for him everywhere.

Three days later, they found him in the Temple, sitting among the doctors, listening to them, and asking them questions; and all those who heard him were astounded at his intelligence and his replies. They were overcome when they saw him, and his mother said to him, 'My child, why have you done this to us? See how worried your father and I have been, looking for you.' Why were you looking for me?' he replied 'Did you not know that I must be busy with my Father's affairs?' But they did not understand what he meant.

He then went down with them and came to Nazareth and lived under their authority. His mother stored up all these things in her heart. And Jesus increased in wisdom, in stature, and in favour with God and men.

THE AGONY IN THE GARDEN

THE SORROWFUL MYSTERIES

THE AGONY IN THE GARDEN (Mark 14: 32–50)

They came to a small estate called Gethsemane, and Jesus said to his disciples, 'Stay here while I pray'. Then he took Peter and James and John with him. And a sudden fear came over him, and great distress. And he said to them, 'My soul is sorrowful to the point of death. Wait here, and keep awake.' And going on a little further he threw himself on the ground and prayed that, if it were possible, this hour might pass him by. 'Abba (Father)!' he said 'Everything is possible for you. Take this cup away from me. But let it be as you, not I, would have it.' He came back and found them sleeping, and he said to Peter, 'Simon, are you asleep? Had you not the strength to keep awake one hour? You should be awake, and praying not to be put to the test. The spirit is willing, but the flesh is weak.' Again he went away and prayed, saying the same words. And once more he came back and found them sleeping, their eyes were so heavy; and they could find no answer for him. He came back a third time and said to them, 'You can sleep on now and take your rest. It is all over. The hour has come. Now the Son of Man is to be betrayed into the hands of sinners. Get up! Let us go! My betrayer is close at hand already.'

THE ARREST

Even while he was still speaking, Judas, one of the Twelve, came up with a number of men armed with swords and clubs, sent by the chief priests and the scribes and the elders. Now the traitor had arranged a signal with them. 'The one I kiss,' he had said 'he is the man. Take him in charge, and see he is well guarded when you lead him away.' So when the traitor came, he went straight up to Jesus and said, 'Rabbi!' and kissed him. The others seized him and took him in charge. Then one of the bystanders drew his sword and struck out at the high priest's servant, and cut off his ear.

Then Jesus spoke. 'Am I a brigand' he said 'that you had to set out to capture me with swords and clubs? I was among you teaching in the Temple day after day and you never laid hands on me. But this is to fulfil the scriptures.' And they all deserted him and ran away.

THE SCOURGING

THE SCOURGING (Matthew 27: 24–26)

Then Pilate saw that he was making no impression, that in fact a riot was imminent. So he took some water, washed his hands in front of the crowd and said, 'I am innocent of this man's blood. It is your concern.' And the people to a man shouted back, 'His blood be on us and on our children!' Then he released Barabbas for them. He ordered Jesus to be first scourged and then handed over to be crucified.

THE CROWNING WITH THORNS

THE CROWNING WITH THORNS (Matthew 27: 27–31)

The governor's soldiers took Jesus with them into the Praetorium and collected the whole cohort round him. Then they stripped him and made him wear a scarlet cloak, and having twisted some thorns into a crown they put this on his head and placed a reed in his right hand. To make fun of him they knelt to him saying. 'Hail, king of the Jews!' And they spat on him and took the reed and struck him on the head with it. And when they had finished making fun of him, they took off the cloak and dressed him in his own clothes and led him away to crucify him.

THE CARRYING OF THE CROSS

THE CARRYING OF THE CROSS (Luke 23: 26–32)

As they were leading him away they seized on a man, Simon from Cyrene, who was coming in from the country, and made him shoulder the cross and carry it behind Jesus. Large numbers of people followed him, and of women too, who mourned and lamented for him. But Jesus turned to them and said, 'Daughters of Jerusalem, do not weep for me; weep rather for yourselves and for your children. For the days will surely come when people will say, "Happy are those who are barren, the wombs that have never borne, the breasts that have never suckled!" Then they will begin to say to the mountains, "Fall on us!", to the hills, "Cover us!" For if men use the green wood like this, what will happen when it is dry?' Now with him they were also leading out two other criminals to be executed.

THE CRUCIFIXION

THE CRUCIFIXION (Luke 23: 33–43)

When they reached the place called The Skull, they crucified him there and the two criminals also, one on the right, the other on the left. Jesus said, 'Father forgive them; they do not know what they are doing'. Then they cast lots to share out his clothing.

THE CRUCIFIED CHRIST IS MOCKED

The people stayed there watching him. As for the leaders, they jeered at him. 'He saved others,' they said 'let him save himself if he is the Christ of God, the Chosen One.' The soldiers mocked him too, and when they approached to offer him vinegar they said, 'If you are the king of the Jews, save yourself'. Above him there was an inscription: 'This is the King of the Jews'.

THE GOOD THIEF

One of the criminals hanging there abused him. 'Are you not the Christ?' he said. 'Save yourself and us as well.' But the other spoke up and rebuked him. 'Have you no fear of God at all?' he said. 'You got the same sentence as he did, but in our case we deserved it: we are paying for what we did. But this man has done nothing wrong. Jesus,' he said 'remember me when you come into your kingdom.' Indeed, I promise you,' he replied 'today you will be with me in paradise.'

JESUS AND HIS MOTHER (John 19: 25–30)

Near the cross of Jesus stood his mother and his mother's sister, Mary the wife of Clopas, and Mary of Magdala. Seeing his mother and the disciple he loved standing near her, Jesus said to his mother, 'Woman, this is your son'. Then to the disciple he said 'This is your mother'. And from that moment the disciple made a place for her in his home.

THE DEATH OF JESUS

After this, Jesus knew that everything had now been completed, and to fulfill the scripture perfectly he said: 'I am thirsty'.

A jar full of vinegar stood there, so putting a sponge soaked in vinegar on a hyssop stick they held it up to his mouth. After Jesus had taken the vinegar he said, 'It is accomplished'; and bowing his head he gave up his spirit.

THE RESURRECTION

THE GLORIOUS MYSTERIES

THE RESURRECTION (John 20: 1–29)

It was very early on the first day of the week and still dark, when Mary of Magdala came to the tomb. She saw that the stone had been moved away from the tomb and came running to Simon Peter and the other disciple, the one Jesus loved. 'They have taken the Lord out of the tomb' she said 'and we don't know where they have put him.'

So Peter set out with the other disciple to go to the tomb. They ran together, but the other disciple, running faster than Peter, reached the tomb first; he bent down and saw the linen cloths lying on the ground, but did not go in. Simon Peter who was following now came up, went right into the tomb, saw the linen cloths on the ground, and also the cloth that had been over his head; this was not with the linen cloths but rolled up in a place by itself. Then the other disciple who had reached the tomb first also went in; he saw and he believed. Till this moment they had failed to understand the teaching of scripture, that he must rise from the dead. The disciples then went home again.

THE APPEARANCE TO MARY OF MAGDALA

Meanwhile Mary stayed outside near the tomb, weeping. Then, still weeping, she stooped to look inside, and saw two angels in white sitting where the body of Jesus had been, one at the head, the other at the feet. They said, 'Woman, why are you weeping?' 'They have taken my Lord away' she replied 'and I don't know where they have put him.' As she said this she turned round and saw Jesus standing there, though she did not recognise him. Jesus said, 'Woman, why are you weeping? Who are you looking for?' Supposing him to be the gardener, she said, 'Sir, if you have taken him away, tell me where you have put him, and I will go and remove him'. Jesus said, 'Mary!' She knew him then and said to him in Hebrew, 'Rabbuni!' – which means Master. Jesus said to her, 'Do not cling to me, because I have not yet ascended to the Father. But go and find the brothers, and tell them: I am ascending to my Father and your Father, to my God and your God,' So Mary of Magdala went and told the disciples that she had seen the Lord and that he had said these things to her.

APPEARANCES TO THE DISCIPLES

In the evening of that same day, the first day of the week, the doors were closed in the room where the disciples were, for fear of the Jews. Jesus came and stood among them. He said to them, 'Peace be with you', and showed them his hands and his side. The disciples were filled with joy when they saw the Lord, and he said to them again, 'Peace be with you.'

THE ASCENSION

THE ASCENSION (Acts 1: 6–11)

Now having met together, they asked him, 'Lord, has the time come? Are you going to restore the kingdom to Israel?' He replied, 'It is not for you to know times or dates that the Father has decided by his own authority, but you will receive power when the Holy Spirit comes on you, and then you will be my witnesses not only in Jerusalem but throughout Judaea and Samaria, and indeed to the ends of the earth.'

As he said this he was lifted up while they looked on, and a cloud took him from their sight. They were still staring into the sky when suddenly two men in white were standing near them and they said, 'Why are you men from Galilee standing here looking into the sky? Jesus who has been taken up from you into heaven, this same Jesus will come back in the same way as you have seen him go there.'

PENTECOST

PENTECOST (Acts 2: 1–16)

When Pentecost day came round, they had all met in one room, when suddenly they heard what sounded like a powerful wind from heaven, the noise of which filled the entire house in which they were sitting; and something appeared to them that seemed like tongues of fire; these separated and came to rest on the head of each of them. They were all filled with the Holy Spirit, and began to speak foreign languages as the Spirit gave them the gift of speech.

Now there were devout men living in Jerusalem from every nation under heaven, and at this sound they all assembled, each one bewildered to hear these men speaking his own language. They were amazed and astonished. 'Surely' they said 'all these men speaking are Galileans? How does it happen that each of us hears them in his own native language? Parthians, Medes and Elamites; people from Mesopotamia, Judaea and Cappadocia, Pontus and Asia, Phrygia and Pamphylia, Egypt and the parts of Libya round Cyrene; as well as visitors from Rome – Jews and proselytes alike – Cretans and Arabs; we hear them preaching in our own language about the marvels of God,' Everyone was amazed and unable to explain it; they asked one another what it all meant. Some, however, laughed it off. 'They have been drinking too much new wine' they said.

PETER'S ADDRESS TO THE CROWD

Then Peter stood up with the Eleven and addressed them in a loud voice: 'Men of Judaea, and all you who live in Jerusalem, make no mistake about this, but listen carefully to what I say. These men are not drunk, as you imagine; why, it is only the third hour of the day. On the contrary this is what the prophet spoke of:

THE ASSUMPTION OF THE BLESSED VIRGIN MARY

THE ASSUMPTION OF THE BLESSED VIRGIN MARY

(Phillipians 3: 20–21)

For us, our homeland is in heaven, and from heaven comes the saviour we are waiting for, the Lord Jesus Christ, and he will transfigure these wretched bodies of ours into copies of his glorious body. He will do that by the same power with which he can subdue the whole universe.

CORONATION OF THE BLESSED VIRGIN MARY

THE CORONATION OF THE BLESSED VIRGIN MARY

(Revelation 12: 1)

Now a great sign appeared in heaven: a woman, adorned with the sun, standing on the moon, and with the twelve stars on her head for a crown.

PRAYERS
OF THE
ROSARY

PRAYERS OF THE ROSARY

THE SIGN OF THE CROSS

IN the name of the Father, and of the Son, and of the Holy Spirit. Amen.

THE APOSTLES CREED

I BELIEVE in God, the Father Almighty, Creator of heaven and earth; and in Jesus Christ, His only Son, our Lord; who was conceived by the Holy Spirit, born of the Virgin Mary, suffered under Pontius Pilate, was crucified; died, and was buried. He descended into hell; the third day He arose again from the dead; He ascended into heaven, sits at the right hand of God the Father Almighty; from there He shall come to judge the living and the dead. I believe in the Holy Spirit, the Holy Catholic Church, the communion of Saints, the forgiveness of sins, the resurrection of the body, and life everlasting. Amen.

THE OUR FATHER

OUR FATHER, who art in heaven, hallowed be Thy name: Thy kingdom come: Thy will be done on earth as it is in heaven. Give us this day our daily bread: and forgive us our trespasses as we forgive those who trespass against us. And lead us not into temptation: but deliver us from evil. Amen.

THE HAIL MARY

HAIL MARY, full of grace; the Lord is with thee: blessed art thou among women, and blessed is the fruit of thy womb, Jesus. Holy Mary, Mother of God, pray for us sinners, now and at the hour of our death. Amen.

GLORY BE TO THE FATHER

Glory be to the Father, and to the Son, and to the Holy Spirit; as it was in the beginning, is now, and ever shall be, world without end. Amen.

The Hail, Holy Queen

Hail, holy Queen, Mother of Mercy! our life, our sweetness, and our hope! To thee do we cry, poor banished children of Eve; to thee do we send up our sighs, mourning and weeping in this valley, of tears. Turn, then, most gracious Advocate, thine eyes of mercy toward us; and after this our exile show unto us the blessed fruit of thy womb, Jesus; O clement, O loving, O sweet Virgin Mary.

V. Pray for us, O holy Mother of God.

R. That we may be made worthy of the promises of Christ.

Let Us Pray

O God, whose only begotten Son, by His life, death, and resurrection has purchased for us the rewards of eternal life, grant, we beseech Thee, that meditating upon these mysteries of the most Holy Rosary of the Blessed Virgin Mary, we may imitate what they contain, and obtain what they promise: through the same Christ our Lord. Amen.

Copies of the *The Rosary Way* are obtainable from McCrimmon Publishing Co. Ltd, your local bookshop, or direct from the Rosary Way Trust.

Enquiries, Donations and Jewellery to:
The Rosary Way Trust,
C/o Miss Hylda Lumsden and Dr. Michael Strode,
Flat 3, The Red House, North Chailey, East Sussex BN8 4JE.
Cheques made payable to the Rosary Way Trust.
Registered Charity No. 800594